Do you remember your husband's favourite hobby?

What did your husband and you like to do during the winter season?

What did your husband and you like to do during the fall season?

What did your husband do a lot that made you laugh?

What was your husband's favourite snack to eat?

How are things being with your children since your husband is no longer around?

What did your husband said he liked the most about you?

What did you promise your husband you will continue to do when he died?

What did your husband and you like to do during the spring season?

What funny story did your husband told you about that made you happy?

Are you still doing all the things your husband taught you to do?

What does your husband's voice sound like?

What did your husband and you liked doing the most together?

Did your husband like any sport and if he did was he good at it?

What would you like to tell your husband that you didn't get a chance to say to him?

Do you remember what favourite clothing your husband liked to wear?

What music did your husband liked to listen to the most?

What did people say they liked the most about your husband?

What did your husband and you like to do during the summer season?

What did your husband say you should do when he died?

If you could change something about how you said goodbye to your husband what would it be?

What was the nickname your husband gave to you?

How are things being with your husband's family since your husband is no longer around?

When your husband was ill at the hospital or at home, how did it make you feel?

What did your husband say about the afterlife?

What do you talk to your son or daughter about after your husband's death?

What do you talk to your siblings about after your husband's death?

What type of drink did he liked the most?

What did you wish you could have said to your husband more often when he was alive?

What gift did you give to your husband that he was really happy to receive?

What favourite snack did your husband get or made for you?

Write down your husband's favourite food?

Write down your favourite memory of your husband?

Have you been feeling differently without your husband being around?

How did you feel when your husband was getting buried?

Did you have a nickname for your husband?

How do you feel about your husband not being around anymore?

Do you remember what favourite shoe your husband liked to wear?

What would you like your husband to know about in the afterlife that you are proud of doing now?

How have your friends supported you after your husband's death?

Made in the
USA
Monee, IL